Get the most from
Social Security

pil
Publications International, Ltd.

Contributing writer:
Lisa Brooks
Cover and interior images:
Shutterstock.com

Louis Weber, CEO
Publications International, Ltd.
8140 Lehigh Avenue
Morton Grove, IL 60053

ISBN: 978-1-64030-783-4

Manufactured in China.

8 7 6 5 4 3 2 1

Table of Contents

Chapter 1
Social Security Basics

Throughout history, humans have relied on some basic sources to ensure economic security. During medieval times, land and labor provided security, with younger members of a family helping to care for older members. In the Middle Ages, guilds were formed to provide employment and financial help to craftsmen and merchants. And in the 1600s, England created what were known as the "Poor Laws" to provide some financial relief to its less fortunate citizens. Colonists brought the ideas in these laws to the New World, and soon America had created some "Poor Laws" of its own. These laws were often harsh and discriminatory, however, and failed to address a situation that we now take for granted: retirement.

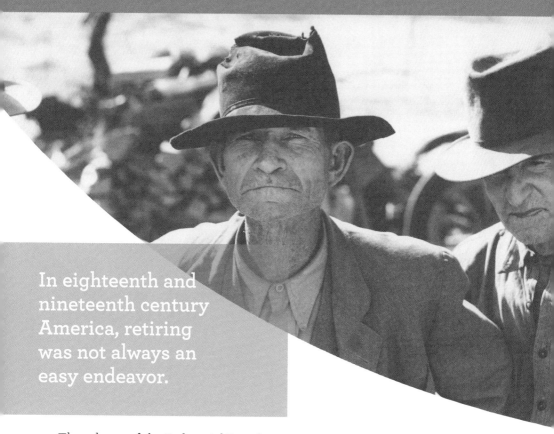

In eighteenth and nineteenth century America, retiring was not always an easy endeavor.

The advent of the Industrial Revolution meant that the country shifted from an agricultural society to an industrial society, and along with that shift, family dynamics also changed. It became much less common for extended family to live together, leaving older Americans with a lack of immediate support.

By the Great Depression in the 1930s, more than half of the elderly in the country were unable to sufficiently support themselves. And even though 30 states had created pension programs by 1935, they were poorly run, and few seniors made use of them. What's more, better medicines and sanitation meant that people were living longer lives, leading to a rapid increase in older Americans by the mid-1930s.

In an effort to provide some measure of relief to the growing population of older Americans in need of financial security, President Franklin D. Roosevelt signed the Social Security Act into law on August 14, 1935.

The act not only included provisions for general welfare, but it also created a social insurance program specifically for retired workers over the age of 65. The main provision regarding this system was called "Title II—Federal Old-Age Benefits," and it stated that payroll tax contributions would be made by employees throughout their working lives, which could then be collected in monthly installments after retirement. This Title II provision eventually became the program that we now know as Social Security.

In 1940, a retired legal secretary named Ida May Fuller became the first person to receive a Social Security check. She received a monthly check for the next 35 years—until she died at the age of 100.

Today, we still pay taxes into the Social Security system, and in return, we receive retirement benefits for the rest of our lives. Although it only replaces about 40 percent of pre-retirement income, Social Security has become an important safety net for older Americans, helping to reduce poverty later in life. It also provides survivors benefits, spouse benefits, and benefits to those who are disabled.

If you are employed, you and your employer both pay into Social Security. You pay 6.2 percent of your earnings, and your employer matches that, for a total of 12.4 percent. (If you are self-employed, you must pay both the employee and employer Social Security tax.) Generally, to be eligible for Social Security you need to work for at least 10 years. But to qualify, you must have earned a total of 40 **"work credits"** throughout your working lifetime. As of 2019, a work credit is defined as a three-month period in which at least $1,360 was earned. Most workers easily surpass this mark, and Social Security calculates the benefit amount based on your highest 35 years of earnings.

Social Security also provides Supplemental Security Income (SSI) benefits to disabled or blind individuals, or those who have limited access to resources. The SSI program makes monthly payments to those who qualify. The income limits to qualify for SSI vary by state, so be sure to call or visit **www.ssa.gov** to learn more about who can apply for SSI in your state.

Also, not all of the income you make is counted toward the limit, including any earnings used to pay for services or equipment needed to help you work, such as wheelchairs or transportation for the blind. Even if you qualify for SSI, you may also still receive aid from your state or county, such as Medicaid, food assistance, or other social services.

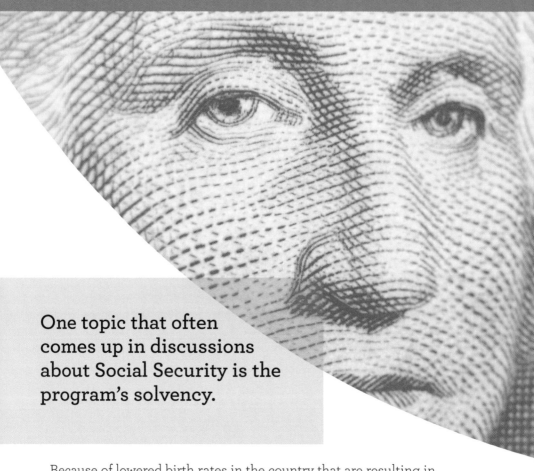

One topic that often comes up in discussions about Social Security is the program's solvency.

Because of lowered birth rates in the country that are resulting in a greater percentage of older Americans, there is often worry that the program will not be able to continue maintaining benefits.

At the moment, it is expected that Social Security benefits will only be payable in full until 2036; so to fix this looming shortfall, lawmakers have proposed different solutions ranging from decreasing benefits to increasing taxes. These adjustments would have the potential to restore solvency for the Social Security program for the foreseeable future.

Chapter 2
Retirement Benefits

A common question on the topic of Social Security is, "How are my benefits calculated?" The most important factor is your "**work record**," also known as an "**earnings record**." Social Security looks at the 35 years in which you earned the highest wages, adjusts them for historical changes, and produces what it calls your "**average indexed monthly earnings**," or "**AIME**." The AIME is calculated using only income up to the maximum taxable earnings—a cap is placed on earnings that are subject to Social Security taxes, and it is adjusted yearly. As of 2019, the limit is $132,900.

Once your AIME has been calculated, Social Security uses a formula to determine what is called your **"primary insurance amount,"** or **PIA**. Your PIA is the amount you'll receive each month from Social Security if you wait until **"full retirement age"** to begin receiving benefits. The specific formula used, as of 2019, is as follows:

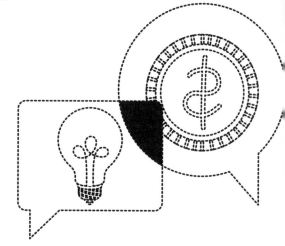

- 90 percent of the first $926 of your AIME,

- Plus 32 percent of any amount between $926 and $5,583,

- Plus 15 percent of any amount over $5,583.

Lastly, Social Security adjusts benefits depending on how old you are when you start receiving benefits. So let's look at how full retirement age and the age at which you begin collecting Social Security can affect your benefit amount.

Before you begin collecting Social Security, you should know your full retirement age, also called **"normal retirement age."**

Many people assume this age is 65; and while that was true for many years, the full retirement age is gradually increasing. The 1983 Social Security Amendments created some changes within the system, including raising the payroll tax to generate a large, short-term surplus of funds to cover the retirement costs of "baby boomers" (generally those who were born between 1946 and 1964). But another way the 1983 Amendments addressed the looming retirement of baby boomers was to slowly raise the age of retirement.

Citing advancements in health care, which increases life expectancy and provides retirees with a better quality of life, Congress raised the retirement age by two months—to 65 years two months—beginning with people born in 1938.

For those born between 1939 and 1942, retirement age again increased by two months every year. For those born between 1943 and 1954, the retirement age was raised to 66 years of age, and starting in 1955, retirement age was raised by two months each year until 1960. Those born in 1960 or later have a full retirement age of 67.

Whether due to longer lifespans or the need to collect full Social Security benefits, one survey found that 30 percent of American workers plan to delay retirement until at least age 70. And as we'll soon see, this tactic may be a smart plan. Depending on when you opt to begin collecting Social Security, you may receive less or more than the full benefit amount.

· ·

Although many workers choose to begin collecting their full Social Security benefits between the ages of 66 and 67 (depending on year of birth), you also have the option of receiving benefits as early as age 62 or as late as age 70.

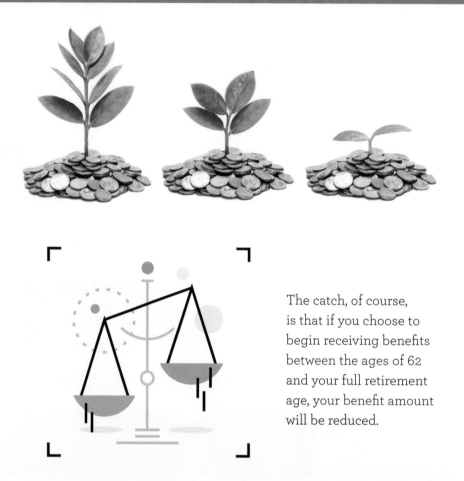

The catch, of course, is that if you choose to begin receiving benefits between the ages of 62 and your full retirement age, your benefit amount will be reduced.

But the opposite is true if you delay your retirement benefits until the age of 70: this results in an increased monthly payment. For instance, if your full retirement age is 66 and your full benefit is $1,000 a month, you would receive $750 a month if you begin collecting at age 62, or $1,320 if you wait until age 70. Many workers find that this extra monthly income is worth the longer wait, but the choice is entirely up to you.

The following chart details the percentage of benefits you can expect to receive depending on when you retire:

Percentage Collected at Retirement Age of

Age Collection Begins	66	67
62	75%	70%
63	80%	75%
64	86.7%	80%
65	93.3%	86.7%
66	100%	93.3%
67	108%	100%
68	116%	108%
69	124%	116%
70	132%	124%

The amount of your monthly benefit depends on your earning history, so the number is different for everyone. To see what kind of benefits you can expect to receive, you can create a personal "my Social Security" account by visiting **www.ssa.gov/myaccount**. Once you sign up, you'll receive estimates of future benefits. You can also review your earnings history, request a replacement Social Security card, and more.

Some people choose to continue working even after they have begun collecting Social Security.

If you choose to receive benefits before your full retirement age but continue working, it should be noted that the amount of your benefit may be reduced.

Social Security places a cap on earnings, and if you earn anything over that cap, you are not considered fully "retired." In 2019, that cap is $17,640 a year; so if you have begun receiving benefits but earn more than $17,640 a year, $1 in benefits will be deducted from every $2 earned over that amount. If, for instance, you earn $25,000 a year—or $7,360 over the limit—$3,680 will be deducted from your benefits.

If, however, you are working in the year in which you'll reach full retirement age, the earnings limit is raised to $46,920, and $1 is withheld for every $3 you earn over the limit. Once you reach full retirement age, there is no limit on what you can earn and still receive full Social Security benefits. And it is important to note that the money deducted from your earnings isn't gone forever: you will recoup the withholdings from your earnings once your full benefits begin. Social Security will increase your benefit to make up for the money that was deducted.

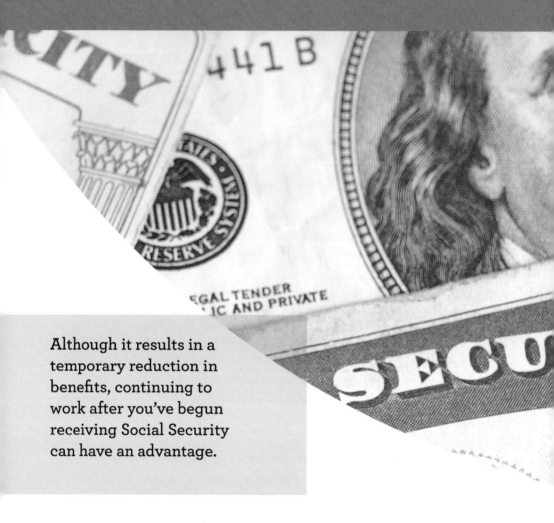

Although it results in a temporary reduction in benefits, continuing to work after you've begun receiving Social Security can have an advantage.

As we have previously seen, Social Security looks at your highest 35 years of earnings to calculate your benefit. If you continue working and some of those highest years of earnings fall within these extra years of employment, they will count toward your ultimate benefit amount. Your lifetime average for monthly income—which is the amount used to calculate your benefit—will be higher, raising your Social Security payout.

Chapter 3
Disability Benefits

No one wants to think about losing their ability to work, but the fact is that around one in four of the young people entering the workforce today will become disabled before reaching retirement age. So it's smart to have a safety net in case the unforeseen happens.

Social Security covers disability benefits in two ways: with **Social Security Disability Insurance (SSDI)** and the **Supplemental Security Income (SSI)** program. SSDI pays benefits to those who are unable to work but have worked long enough to pay Social Security taxes. The SSI program pays benefits to disabled individuals with limited income and resources.

It is important to understand the similarities and differences between SSDI and SSI before applying for a benefits program.

Both SSDI and SSI use the same medical requirements to determine qualifying disabilities, both are managed by Social Security, and both pay benefits when you are unable to work. But SSDI is only available to those who have accumulated a certain number of work credits. The amount of work credits needed depends on your age and the date you become disabled. But SSI is available to individuals who have not accumulated enough work credits, or even to those who have never worked, provided your financial situation demonstrates considerable need.

The following describes the approximate number of work credits needed to qualify for SSDI benefits depending on age:

Age of disability	Work credits needed
Before 24	6 credits or 1.5 years of work over the three-year period before the disability started.
Between 24 and 31	Credits for half of the years between your 21st birthday and the quarter you became disabled. So, if you became disabled at age 29, you would need four years of work, or 16 work credits.
Between 31 and 42	20 credits
Between 42 and 62	Credits are equal to your age minus 12. For example, if you become disabled at age 50, you need 38 credits.
62 or older	40 credits

The SSI program is funded by general tax revenues, unlike SSDI, which is funded by Social Security taxes. SSI is specifically designed to help those who are disabled, blind, or elderly, and who have little to no income.

It provides for basic needs like food, clothing, and shelter. To qualify, you must be over the age of 65, disabled, or blind, and have limited income and resources. As of 2019, the income limit to be eligible for SSI is $771 per month for an individual and $1,157 per month for a couple. Resources, which include cash, bank accounts, land, vehicles, and personal property, cannot exceed $2,000 for an individual or $3,000 for a couple.

Before you can qualify for Social Security disability benefits, you should be familiar with Social Security's definition of disability.

Social Security's definition of disability is stricter than many programs, and temporary or partial disability is not covered. Generally, to be considered "disabled," you must meet several criteria:

1) You can no longer do work that you did before, and your condition significantly limits your ability to perform basic tasks such as lifting, standing, sitting, or walking;

2) You are unable to adjust to a different kind of work; and

3) Your disability has lasted or is expected to last at least a year or is expected to result in death.

To determine whether an individual can be considered disabled, Social Security maintains a list of qualifying medical conditions known as the **"Listing of Impairments."** This list contains conditions, organized by each major body system, that are considered severe enough to qualify for disability, and is divided into two parts:

Part A describes medical criteria for impairments in adults age 18 and over, and **Part B** describes impairments in children. If your medical condition is included in the **List of Impairments**, it is usually a sufficient determination of disability. But if it is not, Social Security may look at other factors to determine whether you qualify for disability.

For detailed information on the disability determination process, visit **www.ssa.gov/disability**.

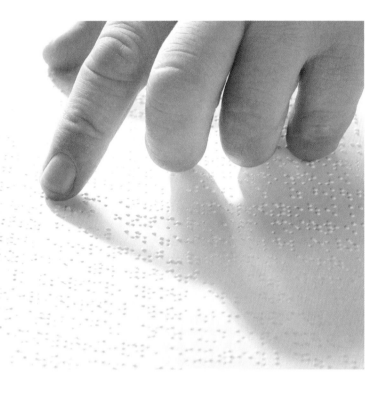

Social Security also provides benefits for certain special situations. The first is for people who are blind or have impaired vision. Social Security considers legal blindness to be vision that cannot be corrected to better than 20/200, or a visual field of 20 degrees or less even with corrective lenses. If vision problems—even if the legal definition of blindness is not met—prevent you from working, you may still qualify for disability benefits. The second special situation is for disabled widows or widowers. If a worker dies, benefits may be paid to their surviving spouse if the spouse is between the ages of 50 and 60, meets the definition of disability, and became disabled either before or within seven years of the worker's death.

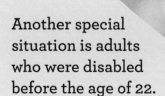

Another special situation is adults who were disabled before the age of 22.

In this case, the adult may be eligible for "child's" benefits paid on a parent's Social Security earnings record. If, for instance, a 66-year-old man begins collecting Social Security benefits and he has a 30-year-old son who has had cerebral palsy since birth, the son is eligible for disabled child's benefits, even if he has never worked. If an adult child is already receiving SSI benefits, they may still be eligible for SSDI disability benefits payable on their parent's earnings record. To be eligible, the adult child must be unmarried, have a disability that began before age 22, and meet Social Security's definition of disability.

Lastly, Social Security provides special benefits to wounded warriors and veterans. Disability claims from military service members may be expedited if they became disabled on or after October 1, 2001, regardless of where the disability occurred.

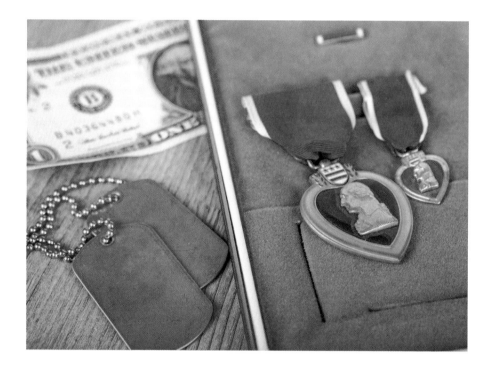

Some veterans are also eligible for both Veterans Affairs and Social Security benefits. For more information on any of these special Social Security programs or to apply for benefits, you can contact Social Security by visiting **www.ssa.gov**, calling their toll-free number at **1-800-772-1213 (TTY 1-800-325-0778)**, or visiting your local Social Security office.

What if you're receiving SSDI or SSI benefits and go back to work?

SSDI recipients are given a nine-month trial work period when they return to work, during which time they continue to receive full SSDI benefits, no matter how much they earn through work. After the trial period, SSDI recipients will lose benefits if they have what's called **"substantial gainful activity,"** or **SGA**. SGA means you are working and earning more than $1,220 per month (or $2,040 if you are blind). For another 36 months, you may still receive SSDI benefits in any month that your earnings fall below the SGA amount.

SSI

SSI recipients may work and continue to receive benefits as long as their wages and resources continue to fall below the eligible limit. However, Social Security may reduce your monthly benefit in proportion to your income. If you stop receiving benefits because your income is over the eligible limit but are later forced to stop working due to disability, your benefits can be reinstated without the need for a new application as long as it is within five years of your first application.

Social Security also deducts the costs of work-related expenses that are needed if you are disabled, such as transportation to and from work, when calculating your benefits. These are known as **impairment-related work expenses** (IRWE).

Chapter 4
Family and Survivors Benefits

When we think of Social Security, "retirement" is often the first thing that comes to mind. But many people don't realize that benefits are also available to children whose parents are retired, disabled, or deceased. More than four million children in the United States receive Social Security benefits, with payments totaling around $2.6 billion a month. In certain cases, stepchildren, grandchildren, and step-grandchildren are also eligible. But not every child who is eligible for benefits receives them, simply because their parents or guardians aren't familiar with the benefits that are available for families. So, who is eligible for these special Social Security benefits?

If you retire, or the unforeseen happens and you become disabled or die, your children may be eligible for Social Security.

To qualify, a child must be your biological child, adopted child, or dependent stepchild, and they must be unmarried and either under the age of 18, or between 18 and 19 and attending secondary school full time. In addition, if you have primary responsibility for a grandchild under the age of 18 whose parents are both disabled or deceased, or if you have legally adopted your grandchild, that child is also eligible for Social Security benefits. If you retire or become disabled, your child can receive up to 50 percent of your full retirement age benefit. If you die, up to 75 percent of your benefit is available.

Although all children in a family can receive benefits, there is a limit to how much Social Security will pay. This limit is known as the **Family Maximum Benefit**.

The Family Maximum Benefit is not a specific number, but rather is calculated as part of your full retirement age benefit. It usually falls somewhere between 150 and 180 percent of your full benefit, and if the total amount of Social Security paid to all family members exceeds this limit, the amount paid to dependents is reduced to stay within the maximum allowable limit. However, if you have a divorced spouse receiving benefits from your work record, that amount is not counted toward the Family Maximum Benefit.

Undoubtedly, you have little control over when you can file for disability or survivors benefits.

However, if there are children in your household who are eligible for Social Security, it could be beneficial to take the initiative of filing for retirement benefits early. Although your overall benefit is reduced when you file early, your children may not receive any benefits until you file. So if, for example, you have two eligible children and your benefit at full retirement age is $2,000 a month, you'll receive $1,500 a month if you file at age 62. But with an approximate Family Benefit Maximum of $3,500, each of your children will also receive $1,000 a month.

When a minor child receives Social Security benefits, these benefits are paid to a **"representative payee,"** or someone who manages the payments on behalf of the child, usually a parent or guardian.

The representative payee is responsible for keeping track of how the benefit payments have been used; the payee must annually report to the Social Security Administration how the money was saved or spent. If the money has been saved, the payee must also list the institution keeping the money and the relevant account numbers. This is because once the child turns 18, any saved money must go back to the Social Security Administration, where it can then be transferred to the adult child.

Another type of Social Security payment is a survivors benefit. Around six million people receive these benefits, which are available to family members after a wage earner has died. They are most often collected by the spouse, former spouse, or children of a worker, with the majority of recipients being widows or widowers. But in some cases, parents, grandchildren, and stepchildren may also qualify.

Survivors benefits are most often based on the amount that the deceased was receiving from Social Security at the time of death, or the amount they would have received if they died before filing for benefits.

The most common recipients of survivors
benefits, widows and widowers, can begin
collecting benefits at age 60—or age 50 if they are
disabled—and, depending on their age, receive between
71.5 percent and 100 percent of their late spouse's Social
Security benefit.

So if, for example, you are 60 years old and your spouse dies at the age
of 55, you can still immediately begin receiving benefits, even though your
spouse hadn't begun collecting benefits. There is an exception if the
survivor is caring for a child of the deceased who is under the age of 16
or disabled. In this case, there is no minimum age to begin collecting
benefits, and the amount is 75 percent of the late spouse's benefit.

If a parent over the age of 62 is financially dependent on a son or daughter who dies, the parent is also eligible for survivors benefits. A single parent can collect 82.5 percent of the deceased's benefit, or two parents can collect 75 percent each. Divorced spouses may also collect benefits when an ex-spouse dies if the marriage lasted for at least 10 years and the beneficiary did not remarry before the age of 60. This applies even if the ex-spouse did remarry. The age and parental status requirements are the same for divorced spouses as they are for widows and widowers.

As with other family benefits, survivors benefits are subject to the Family Maximum Benefit, so if a family's collective benefit exceeds this amount, payments will be reduced to stay within the limit.

It should also be noted that if a widow or widower remarries before the age they are eligible for survivors benefits (either 60 years old or 50 if they are disabled) they can no longer collect survivors benefits. Survivors benefits for widows and widowers were created at a time when it was more common for one spouse to not work. But what if you and your spouse have both worked long enough to have Social Security eligibility?

If you are eligible for both a survivors benefit and a retirement benefit, Social Security does not allow you to collect both benefits at the same time; but it does pay you the higher of the two amounts. You also have the option to collect survivors benefits first, then switch to your own benefits, or vice versa.

For instance, you can begin collecting a survivors benefit at age 60 and delay your own benefits until age 70; or you can file for retirement at age 62 and then later switch to a survivors benefit. As always, the amounts you receive will depend on several factors, including your age and the number of years you worked.

Figuring out the best course of action to take when juggling survivors benefits and a retirement benefit can be confusing, so it's always smart to consult with a retirement planner or financial advisor to decide which path is right for you. There are also Social Security calculators available online, which can give you some insight into how different strategies will work. A few popular choices include:

AARP's Social Security Benefits Calculator
(Bonus: It's free!)
https://www.aarp.org/work/social-security/social-security-benefits-calculator

Maximize My Social Security
($40 for an annual license)
https://maximizemysocialsecurity.com

Social Security Income Planner
($4.99 for a single use, or $49.99 for unlimited use)
https://ssincomeplanner.com

Chapter 5
Applying for Benefits

Once you are eligible for Social Security and have decided it's time to start collecting a payment, the next step is applying for benefits.

Depending on whether you're applying for retirement, disability, family, or survivors benefits, the process can be slightly different. So let's start with the most common of these: retirement benefits.

Around 90 percent of Americans over the age of the 65 collect benefits, with Social Security making up an average of a third of their income. And after paying into the system for your entire working life, it makes sense to recoup some of that hard work.

Before you apply for benefits, make sure you know your full retirement age. For most of us, that's somewhere between 66 and 67.

As we've seen, it can be imperative to know exactly when you are eligible for benefits in order to plan a strategy for retirement. It's also important to note that Social Security cannot process a benefits application filed more than four months in advance. This means that if you would like to begin collecting benefits at the age of 62, you should apply no sooner than when you are 61 and eight months old; similarly, if you'd like to wait to collect until you are 70, you should apply when you are 69 and eight months old.

Once you're ready, there are three ways you can apply for benefits:

- **In person:** If you're unsure of the location of your closest Social Security office, you can use the office locator found on the Social Security Administration's website. Simply visit **https://www.ssa.gov/agency/contact** and click on "Find an Office."

- **Over the phone:** To apply over the phone, call **1-800-772-1213 (TTY 1-800-325-0778)** anytime between the hours of 7 a.m. and 7 p.m., Monday through Friday.

- **Online:** Visit **https://www.ssa.gov/benefits/retirement** to apply online.

Applying is usually simple and can take as little as 15 minutes. But if you apply online, you have the option of saving your application and returning to it at a later date before submitting it.

Although the process is usually easy, there is some information and a few documents you'll want to have on hand to assure things go smoothly. The Social Security Administration recommends that you have the following ready:

- Your birth certificate, a certified copy of it, or some other proof of birth
- Proof of U.S. citizenship or legal immigrant status
- If you're self-employed, you'll need a copy of your W-2 form(s) and/or your tax return for the last year
- Copies of your service papers if you served in the military
- Divorce papers, if appropriate
- Your bank account and routing numbers so funds can be direct deposited
- Social Security number (of course!)

Applying for disability benefits is a bit more daunting than the retirement process, mainly because Social Security needs to weed out fraudulent claims and ensure that your condition meets its definition of "disability."

To improve your chances of being approved and to move the process along more quickly, be sure to gather as many of your medical records as possible.

The Social Security Administration will need to verify the severity of your condition, so it helps to give them a clear picture. You may want to ask your doctor to fill out what's known as a "Residual Functional Capacity Form," which details your condition and your limitations.

Just like applying for retirement, you can apply for disability benefits online, over the phone, or at your local Social Security office.

You'll also need to provide much of the same information that you would supply for retirement benefits, such as date and place of birth, marriage and divorce information, and employment details. But in addition to this basic information, you'll need a list of your medical conditions, detailed information about the doctors and hospitals you've visited, and a description of how your condition has affected your work.

You can find a printable checklist of all the information you may need on the Social Security website: **https://www.ssa.gov/hlp/radr/10/ovw001-checklist.pdf**.

Don't forget to
include a copy of
your doctor's Residual
Functional Capacity Form
with your application.

Many times, a doctor's opinion can sway the decision of the
Social Security Administration. And since, on average, only about a
third of applicants are approved for disability benefits, you'll want to
make a strong case to improve your chances of eligibility.

The Social Security Administration will mail their decision to you, and if
you are denied, you have 60 days to file an appeal. While the appeal process
can be lengthy, the good news is that if your application is later approved,
you can collect retroactive benefits based on your initial filing date.

Applying for family benefits, such as benefits
for children or for a spouse, works much in the same
way as applying for other benefits. You'll need the same kinds
of documents and information—such as birth certificates and Social
Security numbers—for those individuals you'd like to receive benefits.

And again, applications can be filled out online, or you can contact Social
Security by phone or in person. As we've seen, there are generally many
options for applying for Social Security benefits, but one specific type of
benefit—survivors benefits—comes with an exception. Unlike other benefits,
you may not apply for survivors benefits online.

If you are eligible for survivors benefits after a spouse or family member dies, the first step is to notify Social Security of the death.

In many cases, the funeral home will take care of this for you if you provide them with the deceased's Social Security number. But if you need to report it yourself, you must either call or visit your local Social Security office; you cannot report a death online. Once the death has been reported, your circumstances dictate whether you need to apply for survivors benefits. If you were already getting benefits based on your spouse's or parent's work record, you need not apply for new benefits. Social Security will automatically switch your benefits to survivors benefits.

However, if you have been receiving benefits on your own work record, or if you have not been receiving any benefits, you will need to call or visit your Social Security office to apply for survivors benefits (again, you may not apply for survivors benefits online).

In addition to the usual information such as a birth certificate, employment history, and marriage or divorce information, you will need to provide proof of death when applying for survivors benefits. If you have already been receiving your own benefits, Social Security will determine the survivors benefit amount for which you're eligible and pay you the higher of the two. If you have not been receiving benefits, you should begin receiving survivors benefits soon after applying.

Sometimes Social Security applications are denied, with the majority of denied claims being disability applications. However, occasionally retirement or other benefits are denied as well. Reasons for denial can include missing or incorrect information on the application, an application that was filed too early, a lack of work credits, or not meeting an age requirement. If you feel that an application was denied in error, you have 60 days after you receive written notice from the Social Security Administration to file an appeal.

You can get started by completing form SSA-561-U2, **"Request for Reconsideration,"** which is found online at **https://www.ssa.gov/forms/ssa-561.html**.

When you file a request for reconsideration, someone who had no part in the original decision will review your application and send you a new letter explaining their decision.

If you are still not satisfied, there are three more levels of appeal you may use.

The first level is a hearing by an administrative judge. You can request a hearing, as well as download any additional forms you may need, online at **https://www.ssa.gov/forms/ha-501.html**.

You will receive notice of the date, time, and place of your hearing at least 20 days before it is scheduled, and you have the option of appearing by video teleconference as opposed to in person.

If you are not happy with the results of your hearing, the next step is to request a review by the Social Security National Appeals Council in Washington, D.C. You must request a review within 60 days of the result of your hearing by an administrative judge.

For information on downloading and filling out an application to appeal, visit **https://www.ssa.gov/appeals/appeals_process.html** or call or visit your local Social Security office.

While the Appeals Council looks at all applications for appeal, it is possible they may deny your request if they feel that the hearing decision was correct. If you disagree with the Appeals Council, the final level of appeal is to ask for a Federal Court review.

This civil action is filed in the district court of the United States within the judicial district in which you live (or, if you do not live within a judicial district, you may file with the United States District Court for the District of Columbia).

Copies of your complaint must be sent to the Social Security Administration office by certified or registered mail, and you should be aware that there is a fee for filing a civil action in Federal court. It's also important to note that when dealing with Social Security, you have the right to representation by a lawyer, friend, or other qualified individual.

To appoint a representative, you must fill out and sign form SSA-1696, found at **https://www.ssa.gov/forms/ssa-1696.html**.

Chapter 6
Protecting Your Identity

Applying for benefits online can be an extremely convenient way to get the Social Security ball rolling. But there is one very important issue to keep in mind when you're sharing private information online: security. You'll want to prevent any attempts at snooping or identity fraud, so if you apply for benefits online, be sure to use a secure network. If you use a home network that requires a password, that's usually enough. But for even more security, software that includes a firewall and protection against viruses and malware, such as Bitdefender Total Security or Kaspersky Total Security, can provide extra peace of mind. It's best not to enter personal information over an open network away from home, such as in a hotel or coffee shop.

And it's a good idea to think of security when you're away from your computer, too. While there are many instances where it's necessary to reveal your Social Security number—such as to an employer, a bank, or a state unemployment insurance department—there are other times when it's simply not necessary.

Unfortunately, some businesses and institutions do have the right to refuse service or put conditions on services if you refuse to give out your SSN. But if you're not comfortable revealing it, offer an alternative like a driver's license or passport. You also have the right to ask why the number is needed, how it will be stored, and who will have access to the number. You can also ask to see a copy of the business's privacy policy.

There are also some general precautions you can take to protect your number and prevent identity theft. These include:

- **Don't carry your card.** Leave your Social Security card at home, instead of carrying it in a purse or wallet.

- **Invest in a document shredder.** Tossing away documents that contain your SSN makes it easy for thieves to find it. Shred important mail instead.

- **Don't be obvious.** Never type your number into an email or instant message, don't leave a voicemail stating your number, and please, don't ever use your SSN for a password!

- **Be wary.** Never give out your number to a stranger over the phone or to anyone in an unsolicited email. In short, if you're not absolutely certain that someone has the right to your information, keep it to yourself.

If your Social Security card is stolen, be sure to file a report with the police as soon as possible. A lost or stolen card can be replaced, free of charge, by visiting your local Social Security office or applying for a card online.

You'll need to provide your birth certificate or other proof of age, proof of U.S. citizenship, and proof of your identity, such as a driver's license or passport. In some cases, even if you apply online, you'll have to print out your application and take it to your local office to complete the process. But in many cases, you have the option of signing up for a "my Social Security" account. Signing up can not only make it easy to request a new card, but it also gives you personalized information about your benefits and earnings history.

To create a "my Social Security" account, simply visit **https://www.ssa.gov/myaccount/**, fill out some basic information, and choose a username and password.

You'll then be prompted to enter a one-time security code to make sure your information is secure. Once you've created your personal account, you can use it to check the status of benefits applications, sign up for direct deposit for your benefits, change your address, and more. Setting up your own "my Social Security" account is a great way to start exploring your Social Security options.

And while navigating the ins and outs of this system can be a daunting task, hopefully we've provided you with a few tips and tricks to make the transition just a bit smoother.

GLOSSARY:

Average Indexed Monthly Earnings:
Also called AIME, this is the calculation that results from averaging your highest 35 years of earnings, and it is used to determine your monthly Social Security benefit.

Earnings Record:
A record of all earnings you have received throughout your work history that is kept by the Social Security Administration to determine your eligibility for various benefits.

Family Maximum Benefit:
A limit on the amount of Social Security a family can collect on a single worker's earnings record.

Full Retirement Age:
Sometimes called "normal retirement age," this is the age at which you are first entitled to full Social Security benefits.

Impairment-Related Work Expenses:

Also known as IRWE, these are out-of-pocket expenses related to medical supplies, medical devices, service animals, or other items needed by disabled individuals in order to work or to travel from a place of employment.

Listing of Impairments:

A detailed compilation of requirements that Social Security uses to determine disability. Its official name is Disability Evaluation Under Social Security, and it is often informally called the "Blue Book."

Primary Insurance Amount:

Also called PIA, this is the amount a person receives if they begin collecting Social Security at full retirement age.

Representative Payee:

A person who manages Social Security benefit payments for a beneficiary who is incapable of managing his or her own payments, such as a child or disabled adult.

Substantial Gainful Activity: Work that brings in more than a certain dollar amount per month, and therefore disqualifies a person from receiving disability benefits. In order to collect disability, you must be unable to engage in substantial gainful activity (SGA).

Work Credits: The "building blocks" used by Social Security to determine if a person has worked long enough to earn benefits. In 2019, a work credit is given for each $1,360 earned, up to a maximum of four credits per year. Forty credits are needed to qualify for retirement benefits.

Work Record: Another term for "earnings record," as described on page 62.